洞月亮

CAVE MOON PRESS
YAKIMA 中 WASHINGTON

2020

Dedicated to
Ruth Elaine Jutila Chamberlin

Full blooded 99.9% Finn, Filled with Sisui.

Love of my life, life of love for 8 children
each of beautiful hue, combination of races.
She gives each the full wrap of encouragement,
daily prayers, celebrates each life, tears —
she weeps over a lost puzzle piece, Not a day
passes without tears of joy or heartache for her
kids, grandkids, me. Without her love for me
there would be no Milk Train . . .

Appreciation

I introduced Doug to two types of my poems — we called them the hard and the soft. He selected the soft group, felt my soft voice was best, the voice that I know speaks of my journey, pain, suffering, abandonment. I added a poem later, concerned it might not fit. Doug's response: *It fits. It is profound.*

I am so appreciatIve of those words, of his encouragement, the skill and professional detailed attention he has given to Milk Train . . .

© Copyright 2020 Burton Chamberlin
All rights reserved.
Cover Photo: John Huffman
Cover Art: Burton Chamberlin
Book Design: Doug Johnson

ISBN: 978-0-9797785-6-8

Milk Train for Abandoned, Abused, & Aborted

by

Burton Chamberlin

Introduction

My journey is squeezed throughout the book's poems. I wandered through life's pages struggling with abandonment, abuse, pain, confusion – always confusion. Along the way some answers, mentors, seminary, causes to join, friends for support, but always hiding – Do not let the frightened, fragmented kid out of the closet. Do "Let's Pretend" as long as possible? Decades long. Disasters along the way required change and opening the closet a bit. Always trying to make a difference for kids, mine and those we worked with in a number of efforts. Shining a light on the journey's path, Jeremiah's call to run with the horses, and Jesus' call to suffer the children.

Milk Train is dedicated to my love, Ruthie. It was written with her encouragement and PhD re-reads. I survived her "semi-colon, not colon," "whom, not who," and luxuriated in "The poem brought me to tears." I want readers to meet her,
enjoy with me her beauty. Ruthie is 82. I'm 83. She tells me we have another decade, at least, to hold on to each other, and to hold on to our love for Jesus, for truth, justice and freedom for our kids, and those who look like them. And to write.

This book is for folks who are caught in their childhood dramas. Let the pain out, stop hiding, find a safe person to share the trauma, release the demons, say hello to the person in the closet. And raise awareness to support and advocate for abandoned, abused and aborted children.

Table of Contents

Moms Know..9
Moms Do..10
Who Else Knows...11
Mlik Train for Abandoned, Abused & Aborted...........12
No Map to Grandma's House?.....................................16
Care-For..17
Hope Held Hostage...18
Got Shoes..20
Each Morning..21
Graveyards for Unclaimed Children............................22
Suffer the Children or Suffer the Adder......................26
The Great Thumb Shot...29
Caravans Forever...38
Collard Greens on White Bread..................................39
Jesus Extravagant Insurgent..50
Proscribed and Sealed...52
Accused Questions..53
Starved for a Touch...56
Nailed to the World's Last Tree..................................57
To Emmaus...59
Who's Who...62
Hence the Lepidopteran...63
Prosobul..64
Trickle Down..67
Window into Apathy..68
Sun Spots..70
Suffering Succotash...71
Journey...73
Ennui Bawlers...74
Dark Skinned Jew..75
Salinized Well..76
Looking for God..78

Collector of Passions	81
Flash-Backs—Flash Backs	82
Alone	83
Push a Star Ride a Glacier	84
Reticulate	85
I Drink from an Empty Well	86
Intersections	87
Ironic Parameters	89
Who Hears my Heart	90
Taste the Tears	91
Falling Leaves	92
Pray and Park	93
Cherished	94
Sing the Wind's Hosanna	96
There Walks Hope	97
The Silver-Haired Socialist Aristocrat	100
Care-Taking — by Crow	102
God's Garden in the Desert	105
What Worth a Man at 80	108
Sixty	110

MOMS KNOW

I remember how childhood tussles
    got resolved in my neighborhood.
How squabbles did not lead to
    'sticks and stones' ambushes.
How a bloody nose did not set loose
    a fire-storm on the block.
Somehow a call went out to the peacemakers.

From front porches up and down the street
    the call for peace blared from shrieking moms
        and my grandmother.
    Melvin, Fredrick, Helen, Gerald,
    Robert Junior, Rebecca Anne.
    Get your little butts home right this minute!

Justice was meted quickly, dispassionately, with no impunity.

The message:
    Stop the war fix the problem
    If you caused the fight
    Go say you're sorry.

You would sometimes find your antagonist at the door.
    Tell him you're sorry you bloodied his nose said the mother.
    I'm not sorry 'cause he hurt my feelings. He deserved it.
    But I want to be his friend and won't hit him again.
    And then Rebecca Anne went home.

MOMS DO

Moms who work day and night jobs
Pushing mops and making shakes.
We kids get to eat, wear clean clothes,
Get shots, second-hand lap-tops,
Wake-up to eggs or Cap'n Crunch,
She never misses morning hugs
Sneak a hello get a chicken nugget
plus a signature for school trip.
Too often scary adults ask
Where's your Mom?

Working her butt off for us.

WHO ELSE KNOWS

Sitting in a pew, in a classroom, in a foster home,
who sees her heart's scars, the jagged journey's signature?
The rejected abandoned girl carries memory tomb-stones
around her neck. Many colliding stones of abuse, of fear.
What does she hear, see, feel?

She hears the cries from the cages.
She sees their bruises, torment, blank stares.
She feels their once happy hearts dying without hope.
She cries, she screeches "Why?" for the children, and
"Why?" for herself.

MILK TRAIN FOR ABANDONED, ABUSED & ABORTED

Got on a train in Little Rock, years ago,
      my daddy gave Mr Porter ten silver dollars
      to take care of me, keep me fed and safe,
      make sure I got off at grandma's town.
      I was five then, didn't see my daddy
      till I was ten.

The train? A slow Milk Train, stopped all the time,
      filling up with kids ages three to thirteen.
      Hundreds. Black, white, Mulatto, Latins
      from Miami, some from Cuba, and places we
      never heard of. A living geography lesson. We
      stopped to pick up more kids, their names,
      where they came from, we couldn't pronounce.

Mr Porter was in charge. Nobody ever gave
      more hugs, understood more languages,
      cried more hearing each kid's story. Each
      of us got a "You special and don't you forget it!"
      To make sure how special we were, he'd say
      our name. "You special Miss Lindsey, and don't
      you forget it!" No kid on the Milk Train got lost
      or forgotten. That was a big change for all
      of us, cause we — each one of us — had been
      lost, forgotten, abused, abandoned, aborted.

Aborted? "Yes," answered "Nobody," one of the older kids.
      His name he said was given to him by folks who
      didn't give a damn if he lived or died. Told he was a
      worthless piece of shit. He was a nobody. Mr Porter,
      relentlessly kept telling "Nobody" he was "Somebody."

'Who are aborted?" I asked. "Kids here on the Milk-Train?"

We knew when "Nobody" had a speech to make.
    He stood up and swept his audience
    with glaring eyes. Not yet healed "Nobody"
    was still very angry.

'Who? Who? We who were abandoned at birth.
    Who were warehoused, were sold!
    We who are multi-colored, mixed,
    We the "hard-to-adopt," the rejected.
    We who were fostered and lost.
    And we who were jailed!
    Our lives were aborted! Like
    Space rockets when prevented
    to launch: Abort! Abort! Exhausted
    "Somebody" turned around and fell into
    Mr Porter's arms.

No one asked Mr Porter, "Where we going?"
    "We there yet?" Every time the train
    stopped we got anxious. Big audible
    sighs exploded as new kids squeezed in.
    What did we know? We were safe.
    Mr Porter loved us — all of us.
    Not one kid had bruises on her
    face or arms. No kid cried himself
    to sleep. We changed. We once were
    survivors — did whatever necessary
    to survive. On the train we were no
    longer bullies, gossips, liars, thieves.
    We had hope. We helped Mr Porter
    take care of each other. We listened
    to the stories, the fears, the beatings,

the sexual abuse, the loneliness, the
wondering would anyone ever
love us like Mr Porter loved us?
Was Mr Porter an angel?

Sissy, older at thirteen, was big sister to
　　the younger girls, some boys
　　hoped she would be their mother.
　　Sissy was pregnant. Raped by her
　　step-father, thrown out by her
　　mother, now so thankful to be on
　　the Milk Train she often cried out
　　of joy.

Sissy told Mr Porter and those near-by,
　　her baby was talking to her. Her girl-
　　baby told Sissy, womb babies were
　　connected and shared stories. They
　　were upset, reported Sissy's girl-baby.
　　"What's with this war outside between
　　pro and anti abortion folks?" The babies
　　wanted to know if the war is really about them.
　　Do they really care about us, love us,
　　or use us to get votes. Sissy's girl-baby
　　reported the wee-ones in wombs weren't
　　coming out till war got settled.

Then, one time someone did ask, "Where
　　are we going? Do we have to get off?"

Get off we did.
　　Mr Porter led us to an amphitheater,
　　deep in the mountains, "Rockies" he

called them. Surrounded by trees
we sat surrounding Mr Porter. Eyes
from the trees watched, furry tails,
antlers, big paws! All mesmerized.
What an amazing gathering. Mr
Porter opened his arms and closed
them around all of us.

Mr Porter appeared to speak to each of us,
gentle whispers. "Look around dear
children, your beauty is celebrated by
by God's beauty. The trees sing to you.
The flowers bathe you in sweet fragrances.
You see the eyes of fellow creatures
telling you they love you. Love them
back, keep them safe."

We didn't get back on the Milk Train.
At least I didn't. I didn't see Mr Porter again,
not in living color, always in my heart, his
words and hugs and tears constants. Healed?
Still healing, but now loving my own adopted
children. Where did all the Milk train kids go?
"after Somebody." Sissy? Where did Mr Porter go?
I hope he is still on the Milk Train loving
abused, abandoned and aborted kids.

NO MAP TO GRANDMA'S HOUSE?

At holiday we need a store that sells fantasy maps.
    Directions to find where we come from.
    How to get to grandma's house.
The visible world answers almost all the questions
    But never answers my really big question
    Why me?
Who decided I should get plopped out on the world stage?
What kind of planning went into let's make a baby?
Apparently the event was triggered by
    Spontaneous urgency and
    Oops to uncontrolled passion.
As a ward of the court I have case workers
    Case-workers remind how fortunate
    I am not to have been aborted.

Back to the need for a fantasy map.
    If the family tree is barren
    If your birth certificate calls you Baby Girl
    If Thanksgiving offers no plane ticket or name place

Then you are fortunate
    You get to make it up!
And if you're very fortunate
    Your new map will
    Stork a new life
    Guarantee a name place
    Lead to an orchard!

CARE-FOR

Not a child, a parent, an invalid, a totterer,
       not a nurse's aid, a mate who watches
       over her dementia partner, a diaper
       changer of bed-ridden, a cleaner
       of cages. Not one who is cared-for
       or who cares-for doesn't know
       the challenge, endurance, patience,
       eyes that cry for a touch.

Who intervenes before the care-giver
       cares too much?

HOPE HELD HOSTAGE

Look in the eyes of
One abandoned child
Moribund nothing

Look in the eyes
Children with dead eyes
Empty resignation

Her eyes searching
Heart squinting
Hoping yet hopeless

Searching cathedral opus
Words of hope or death
Stop killing the fetus
Roars the well of the Congress
While voting against WIC
Food stamps, shelters
Hope yields to death

Then to challenge
Ranting congressmen. You
Adopt hard-to-place child
Then death yields to hope
Then fetus has hope

The conversation changes
See the rhetoric through
Eyes of the once abandoned
Now rescued safe loved child
The debate will change to
Save the child every child
Save born and unborn
Death yields to Hope

GOT SHOES

All God's children got shoes!
        No, they all don't got shoes!
        A lot of them don't got moms,
        Or dads, or homes. or any
        Place to lay their heads.
        Not even a manger.

EACH MORNING

Kneeling, praising God for his new mercies
Kneeling, praying selfish protection for my
Black, Brown, Yellow children,
they will not be stopped while driving,
nor be shot because of their color, nor
because they are articulate and outspoken.

Kneeling for justice for all children
Black, Yellow, Red and White,
hoping and praying they are
all precious in His sight!

GRAVEYARDS FOR UNCLAIMED CHILDREN

I walk through canyons of dry bones and ashes
Skeletal archives of wars past and future.
      Graveyards for unclaimed children.

Mounds of bones no headstones.
Skulls with neat bullet holes.
Shattered arms and legs.
      Tiny limbs that never crawled.

The ashes swirl sucking pulling down.
Furious flurries sting my face.
Eyes with no faces appear.
Cacophony of children's whisperings

      We cried for help from
      hundreds of valleys of death,
      from barbed-wire fences.
      Where were you?
      Where was God?

I scurry now scrambling toward safety clawing escaping.
Dust cakes my eyes voices follow pleading

      Do not forget us
      It will happen again
      It is happening now
      Help us.

Finally out of the valley.
The Whisperings haunt my heart.
The Questions nauseate.

But why me?

>	I didn't know about the killing.
>	I did know some of it.
>
>	But I didn't know the extent.
>	The continual slaughter of innocents.
>	I couldn't do anything to stop it.

Now standing above timbre-thumping bones.

My lungs retching. I hear screaming.
Where?

My mind!

>	How did my mind become a courtroom?
>	How did I become the single defendant?
>
>	I'm not alone in this.
>	I was asleep along with generations of
>	Insouciant grape-teethers.

My complaining denial is interrupted:

>Do not forget us
>It will happen again
>It is happening now
>Help us!

Am I branded with this dirge?
Certainly there are others who are
Best equipped to speak for the dead.
Mellifluous voices to enjoin the
Public to stop killing children.

And what about the ultimate defendant!

>Where was God?

The question has a
Thousand interrogators,
God in the dock.
Immutable yet mute.
Prescient yet distant.

I stand over the canyon.

I tremble at question's urgency.
It is now my question.
Where are you God?
Suffer the children you said
Yet they suffer.

If not God who is their advocate?
If not God who is their protector?

I rage at the inadequacy of my supplication.
I seethe furious at this God who
Seemingly abandoned children.
I hesitate demanding redress.
I lean into the abyss and cry

    GOD! Answer the question!

And the answer comes back
It is a "still small voice."

    Do not forget them
    It will happen again
    It is happening now
    Help them!

SUFFER THE CHILD OR SUFFER THE ADDER

Sweet child,
    Hollered the harridan from hell.
    Look down from your redoubt.
    Here I am under your castle of wood.
    I have been sent to bring you out.
    You're old enough, age eight. I thought you understood.

Sweet child,
    You must abandon your alembic rope.
    It cannot take you to a land of hope?
    Now put on your St Audrey's Lace.
    Climb down the ladder,
    Or suffer the adder.
    But first rouge your face.

Terrible person,
    Whoever you are, go away.
    You sound nasty and cruel.
    I'm not about to go your way.
    I may be a child but not a fool.

Terrible person,
    Who says I have to leave my fort?
    Who says I have to wear cheap lace?
    Who says I have to rouge my face?
    Listen deceiver to my retort!

Sweet Child
>   It's me your auntie,
>   No need for fright.
>   Trust me sweet girl,
>   For I will take you
>   To a world of delight.

Terrible person
>   I remember you now,
>   You stole my sisters
>   Promising them security
>   You ravaged their purity.

Sweet Child
>   To me you have been sold
>   Your mother's receipt I hold.
>   You see you have no choice
>   From now on I am your voice.

Terrible person
>   The world has spoken.
>   Your grip on me is broken.
>   The law cannot be denied.
>   Justice is now on my side.

Dear Child,
>   There is no law here.
>   I have nothing to fear.
>   No newsmen to report.
>   No jailers no court.

Terrible person
>	You assume I have no power.
>	I spit on you this very hour.
>	You think I rely on an imaginary rope.
>	What did you call it? Alembic hope?
>
>	Look! Here comes a redemptive sight.
>	Not a rope, but a feathered carpet for my flight.
>	A garland of doves will free me from your grasp.
>	Beware the adder who plots your final gasp.

THE GREAT THUMB SHOT

Civics class was played on dirt.
>Draw a circle 24 inches in
diameter. Players emptied a
small bag spilling marbles
before knees. Each rolled
out a shooter.

The shooters were Steelies,
>and they were deadly.
A winning thumb-shot
would inflate your
power, and prestige,
now known as swag,
and fill your bag!

Teams were formed long before
>we were born. We were
divided by bicycles; our
side had crappy second
hand bikes; we played
against shiny Schwinn
riders, guys from ritzy homes.
Marbles also divided us.

Our marbles - Aggies, Galaxies,
>and clay Commies - these
cheapies filled our bags.
"Commies?" Not a clue.
Long before the red threat.

The Schwinn boys had exotic marbles,
    beauties called Alleys, lots of
    different kinds with nifty names —
    Spiral, Ribbon, Bumblebee, Corkscrew.
    They played with Puries, all glass
    blues, purples, so clear you
    could see through them. Alleys
    were used to entice us to give up a
    Steely. If you beat 'em out of a
    couple bumblebees, you picked
    up your marbles and pedaled home
    as fast as you could. Most of
    the time the Schwinn boys didn't
    care how many Alleys they lost.
    "We got more where they came
    from." Rich and cocky. It seemed
    we fought those guys for the rest
    of our lives.

Rules were written in the dirt we played on.
    No one argued with basics.
    Five teams, five shooters each
    with two subs. Five "games" like
    sets in tennis made a game, the
    winner won the most marbles by
    "shooting" the opponents marbles
    out of the circle. The ante, 5 marbles,
    placed strategically in the circle.
    If a shooter's Steely missed its
    target and stayed in the circle, it

was fair to try to knock it out of
the circle. If the other side did
hit it out, the "game" was over, the
other side kept the Steely and all
the marbles left in the circle. Nobody liked that rule.

The teams were made-up of the best shooters.
The Schwinns had 3 scary-good ones.
Our side had 1, the best of all, could
beat their 3 any time. Our best could
only play one "game," and beat their
best — five marbles for us. Their 2
good shooters could usually beat
our next best, and they would have
a 2-1 advantage, ten marbles to five.
So it came down to how the lessers
would win or lose; it was a toss up,
until one day one of our subs beat our
best! Little Sister had developed the
best thumb shot ever. Fierce competitor,
she beat everyone on our team, including
her brother, and gobbled up our Steelies.
The Schwinns said no way would they
let a girl play. Little Sister said she
would show them! She didn't watch
the games after the Schwinns cut her
out. We didn't fight for her. She called
us names, "weak weenies" was the worst.
But we had to keep playing.

We traded, made deals sometimes
        with a Schwinn boy that would
        cause a fight that would bomb the
        circle, that would scatter the marbles.
        Little brothers would stuff marbles in
        their pockets and run to our clubhouse.
        We loved to play and did until Maggot appeared.

Maggot was a bully, older, bigger, and nasty.
        He would always sneak up on us, then he
        would scream — "You little shits!" and
        stomp on the marble circle and throw
        punches. We knew he would scream first,
        so we jumped out of his way, but we
        would crash into those behind us.
        Maggot kept screaming, running to
        pick up one of our crappy bikes,
        tossing, sometimes smashing it.
        He would run off, swearing, laughing.
        We would return to the game, happy
        to be safe, no bruises or cuts. We
        would look for our marbles,
        especially the Steelies. Could not
        find them. Maggot never messed
        with Schwinn bikes. We would get
        angry and tell the Schwinn guys we
        quit, and they would tell us not to
        worry, they would take care of him.
        And we would play for several more
        weeks before he attacked again.

Maggot was a big problem, our problem.
Little Sister named him for a slimy
dead fly. Where did he come from?
Why does he mess with us? And not
Schwinns? Is he paid some bucks to
go after us? Is he somebody's brother?
None of us had a big brother. Our
folks would close down the games,
especially afraid for our younger
brothers and sister. We asked a
bunch of questions: how would
cops find him and stop him? How
would the president stop him?
Wow, that stopped us. Ike squashed
the Germans to stop the war.
Except voting in our class for Ike for
president, we knew nothing about
government, and we were sure we
couldn't call the president to help us
squash Maggot.

We knew we needed a plan. We didn't know
how to make a plan. Somebody said,
"Maybe we all jump on him next time
he comes. We beat him up!" Another:
"Think of the way we play marbles. we
drop a Steely in the center of the circle,
to get the Schwinns to go after it.
We do the same to entice Maggot. We
use all our Steelies to get him to the
game. We trap him!" Lots of responses.
"You want us to use ALL our Steelies.

No Way!" Another: "He will scatter our
marbles and our Steelies and then run."
How do we set the trap for Maggot?
What do we want if we catch him?
Little Sister was listening, sitting way
in the back of the clubhouse. She
erupted: "You set the trap. I'll get him!"

Boy did Little Sister get him, but she got
    clobbered first, broke her arm, and
    split her chin wide open, 15 stitches.
    The trap worked like a charm.
    We told the Schwinns our parents
    wouldn't let us play anymore, too
    dangerous, they were afraid one of
    the small kids would get hurt. But . . .
    we wanted to play one last game,
    the biggest game of our lives, and
    we would only use our Steelies. The
    Schwinns could hardly cover their
    grins. We set the game for the next
    Saturday.

Maggot showed up when we rolled out
    our Steelies. He came charging
    yelling "Little shits" at us and
    kicked our Steelies toward the
    Schwinn's side, while swinging
    his fists towards us. We ducked
    and ran. Maggot kept yelling,

and laughing and ran down the
alley. The Schwinns got our
Steelies. Little Sister got
Maggot. Well, Maggot got
Little Sister, that's how she
got hurt, but she did find out
who he was, and nailed him!

Little Sister found Maggot's bike
at the end of our alley.
She moved it across the
street next to the bus stop.
When Maggot came running
down the alley he saw
Little Sister with his bike
at the bus stop. He yelled,
"She's a thief, stop her, she
stole my bike." He ran at
her, scared her, the bus
was beginning to stop,
but she ran in front of it
and the bus hit her and
knocked her to the street,
blood spilling from her chin.

Little Sister sat up crying.
Maggot knew trouble was
coming and tried to get away.
Two women, mothers, grabbed
him and held him. An ambulance
took Little Sister to the hospital,
the police took Maggot to his
parents' house.

Our parents wanted Maggot arrested.
    After a big meeting with all the
    parents — ours and Schwinns,
    it was decided that Maggot -
    Charles - would be sent to live
    with his grandparents and could
    not return. Charles' parents paid
    Little Sister's medical bills.
    Maggot's brother was a Schwinn
    rider, who was grounded forever.
    We got back our Steelies.

Little Sister's cast was as an autograph
    book; she didn't ever want
    to take it off. It covered her
    right arm, her fingers sticking
    out, waving and poking. Her
    thumb was free; she could
    still clobber us and take away
    our Steelies with her thumb shot.

We would meet in our clubhouse and
    often talk, more like laugh, over
    Maggot's punishment, our knocking
    out the Schwinns. Little Sister,
    if she was there, would break
    into our laughing. "OK, boys,"
    with emphasis on boys,
    "what did we learn?" We were
    hopeless. "Don't play with rich
    Schwinn guys. Find a Maggot
    to fight for us!' Little Sister stopped
    asking.

She became the first women mayor
of our town.

CARAVANS FOREVER

Hey, you alone? Where're your parents?
    Don't know. Somewhere in front, maybe.
Better find 'em. Get left behind get kidnapped!
    What? Who's gonna steal a ten-year-old kid?
Your folks got enough to make this trip.
Then they got enough to buy you back.
    How come you telling me this stuff?
You're a good kid. I don't want you taken.
I work with them. Get money when I . . .
    . . . when you what? Grab me?
If they get you, and your folks don' pay,
You ain't gonna get to where you're going.
You need to run! Find your parents.
Trouble coming.
    Holy Moses! I'm gone . . .

COLLARD GREENS ON WHITE BREAD

This is a poem about my Nellie,
who raised me in the deep South
in the early '40s, from when I was three until five.
She was beautiful, a black woman who
mothered me while my mother
was in hospital. She taught me
how to be a little-man, as she called me.
She asked me never to use the
N-word, because it made her
so very sad.

Don't go out in the street in front of your house
tomorrow! Especially in the morning. Stay inside!

Why?

Don't you know anything?
Cecil was always telling me things I didn't know.
Or things he didn't think I knew.
Anyway, he was older, and assumed he was boss.

You don't know nothing 'cause you were born up
north. Not your fault. You talk right fine southern
now, but you got a thick brain so I got to catch you
up on stuff. Cecil said stuff instead of things when
he was excited.

We lived on Maple as long as I could remember.
Since I was three and that seemed long enough
to know something about living on Maple
and there was certainly nothing scary I knew going
on out in the street.

Cecil was six so I thought he probably knew something
about living on Maple I didn't know. He lived three
houses down on the other side of the street. He said he lived
there forever.

Again: Why?

Huh? Cecil was still thinking about my thick brain.
Why shouldn't I go out in the street tomorrow?

Why? Why? Cecil was getting excited.
Boogeyman, you big dummy. Boogeyman!

Boogeyman? I'd never heard of it before.
What's a Boogeyman Cecil?

He's coming Tuesday morning in a truck.

He's new here so you ain't ever seen him before.
He comes to steal your garbage and if you're out
front, he'll steal you!

Thick brain or not I understood Cecil.
I was scared silly. I took an immediate oath.
Never would I go out in the street on Tuesdays.
Not as long as I lived on Maple.

But I did peek out the window
that Tuesday morning.
Sure enough there came the truck.
Out stepped a tall powerful Negro.
And sure enough he stole our garbage.
He threw our garbage bag in the truck.
Then my stomach jumped.
My brain flew into high speed fear.
The Boogeyman was a Negro!
He steals garbage and little boys!
Frozen behind the curtain I watched.
The Negro got back into the truck
and drove down the street.
I then realized I had peed my pants!

Nellie, I screamed! Nellie!
Thank God Nellie was in the house.
She would save me from the Boogeyman.
Nellie was my guardian she took care of me.
My daddy was on the road during the week,
and some weekends. Selling flour.
Nellie was always there when he was gone.
My real mom was in the hospital.
Nellie was something like a mom
But of course she wasn't.

She made sure I was clean each day,
fed me all the time. I liked everything
except collard-greens on white bread.
When I cried she tucked me under her
bosoms and held me close until I was ok.
She wasn't my mom but I sure loved her.

Nellie! Help!

Nellie burst through the kitchen door.
She looked at my eyes then my pants.
Lord, my little-man. What's wrong?

Boogeyman I yelled!
Boogeyman stole our garbage!
If I was out there he would've stole me!
I was sputtering now but could not let go . . .
Boogeyman!!! And I started to cry.

Nellie's arms corralled me, again
tucked me under her bosoms,
safe now, warm and protected.

Now child, who's putting this Boogeyman
mumbo jumbo in your head? Sounds like
it's coming out of Cecil's mouth. That so-called
Boogeyman is the new garbage collector.
He comes every Tuesday. And child I know him.
He's a wonderful man, a father and a
Deacon in my church, a fine Christian!

Blurting out now. Cecil said the Boogey . . .
I dropped the rest. Cecil said he stole little boys
like me. And Nellie. The man is a Negro! A Negro!

Nellie squeezed me tight then gently pushed me away.
Dear child you are so sweet and so ignorant.
You live such a sad life not knowing many colored.
Look at me child. What do you see?

My Nellie.

Your Nellie is a Negro a Negress.
You see me as your Nanny, your
sandwich maker, your protector.

Never a colored. Do you child?
Gulping, No ma'm just my Nellie.

Child the garbage man does not steal . . .
little boys or garbage. And he's no
Boogeyman. His name is Mr. Johnson.

But what about Cecil?

Cecil should be taken to the woodshed.
But please child don't tell him I said so.

Why?

Cause I could lose my job and your
Nellie wouldn't be here for you.

Who would take you away?

Leave it be child. We're fine here.
And so is Mr. Johnson. Now your daddy's
gone for the weekend. You come to church
with me come Sunday. OK?
Yes, ma'm.

TWO

Weeks later maybe months,
I don't remember how long.
But everything changed. Life changed.
My Nellie was gone. I was on a train.
Going back up north, my daddy said,
your grandma will take care of you!

Seems my real mama lived in the hospital.
Once in while I would go with daddy.
I don't ever remember seeing her there.

This one night we came home late and
It was real dark scary no moon dark.
The street light was down at Cecil's.
His daddy was a policeman and I guess
he needed the light more than we did.

Our house was surrounded in the back
by sticky thorny blackberry bushes.

They were so close that when the wind blew

the bushes would scratch the walls.
Once I climbed out my bedroom window.
Landed right in the middle of the bushes.
Got stuck! Nellie got me out. She got
stickers stuck in her arms and hands.
She was not happy with her child.

Anyway that night coming home from the hospital
we were getting out of the car when daddy
grabbed me by the neck and pulled me back.
Hurt like heck.

Somebody's in the house. Hear 'em?
I could hear feet stomping like warning us.
You run down to Cecil's and tell his daddy.
I'll wait here, try to catch him if he comes out.
Now run!

And run I did. What came next is a blur.
But what I do remember is me, Cecil, Linda Sue
and the Wilcox kids from way down the street.
We were all way out in back behind my house.
Mr. Wilcox was protecting us but he was also
telling us to watch carefully cause he and
the neighbors along with my daddy,
they were gonna catch a coon.

Cecil, I whispered, what does he mean?
Why so many guns?

Cecil hissed at me. You big dummy.
We're gonna catch that Boogeyman!
We're gonna shoot a Negro!

I got sick. I didn't pee my pants.
I wanted to throw-up but I couldn't.

Cars were parked on our front lawn.
At a horn signal the car lights were
turned on. The house was bright with
light. Then men got out of the cars.
Cecil's daddy yelled, Come on out!
If you don't come out now
we're coming in to get you!

The back window opened and out came
the Negro. He was trying to sneak out the
back, but I knew he would get caught in the
blackberry bushes.

Quiet kids whispered Mr. Wilcox.
Watch this, whispered Cecil.

The man fought through the bushes.
When he emerged lights came on from
cars parked behind the house.

Put up your hands someone yelled.
He didn't, he tried to run. Several shots
fired. He fell.

All right kids. Follow me said Mr. Wilcox.
He led us toward the man on the ground.
I did not want to go. Cecil pushed me.
C'mon we get to see a dead coon.

When we got close and could see the blood
I did throw up.

I went back to the spot we watched from.
I could hear Cecil's daddy. Remember
children this is what you do when a Negro
invades your home.

I wanted Nellie. She would explain this to me.
She would hold me, tell me all would be fine.

But I would never see Nellie again.

After that night nothing would be fine.
Cecil told me the man that was shot
he was the Boogeyman who stole our
garbage. But I knew that was a lie.

My daddy? He didn't say anything about the
shooting. He did tell me it was time to
leave the South, time to go north.
He never answered why I couldn't see Nellie.
I kind of knew she couldn't come to the house,
couldn't take care of me after the shooting.

People put the squeeze on my daddy. Get rid of her!
I did learn daddy couldn't afford a white nanny
And that's why we went north to live with grandma.

I didn't like him for taking me away from my Nellie.
He must have known she had too much influence on me. I
think he was a little afraid of her.

Nellie said he was a nice man. She never said bad about
him not that I remember. But I knew she believed my
daddy didn't like Negroes and that made her sad.
She told me that when I went to church with her.

THREE

That Sunday morning long before the shooting
is a very clear memory. I have no idea
how we got to Nellie's church. I don't
remember how we got into the church,
I do see the pew we sat in, the glistening white
walls that surrounded the folks.
The folks? All Black. Men, women, and lots of kids.
They stared at me something awful. They all sang
and sang and sang. Not a word I recall,
but the magic of the music filled my heart
deep so very deep, even to this day.
Nellie let me stand on the pew when folks
stood to sing. She rocked, the entire pew rocked,
the church rocked.

A man talked for hours. I slept through most of it.
We went to the basement and ate chicken.
Still smell it, taste it. Mr. Johnson took me to the men's
bathroom. He laughed when I closed the door
to the stall. After I washed, he took my hand
and led me to Nellie.

When we got to her I could see Nellie's tears.
She had been crying. She was surrounded
by several women. I knew scold when I saw it
and these ladies were scolding Nellie.
When they saw me they stopped,
several walked away. Mr. Johnson patted
Nellie on the arm, nodded to me and disappeared.
Nellie looked down at me, wiped tears and
gave me a hug. "Who would think one little white boy
would start such a fuss. Let's go home."

Later she told me the ladies were angry with her for
bringing me to church. Nellie said they weren't liking
me anymore than daddy liked Negroes.
And they spurned her to think she could
change the world by bringing
a little white runt to their church.
But it was fine she purred.
The two of us would do just fine.

JESUS EXTRAVAGANT INSURGENT

Irreverently called the
Religious establishment
Irrelevant.

Attacked the religious as vacuous profiteers
Makers of mega-carnivals
Sellers of cheap seats to
Heaven.

Declared theocracy demonic
Declared the widow
The alien the orphan
His family.

Called scaled-back seekers to be
Fishers for the new kingdom.
Told his fishers to disregard
Polity politeness.

Told the polity pious
They were accountable for every child
 Who cried because of hunger,
 Who screamed because of rape,
 Who wailed for murdered mothers,
 Who slept in dumpsters.

No surprise the political suits wanted him silenced,
Called him a threat to security,
A dangerous provocateur.

No surprise the pew suits
Flooded the air with innuendo,
With doubt regarding his birth,
He traveled with loose women,
He associated with vigilantes.

No surprise the proper suits
Clamored for his removal.

No surprise when "Remove him"
Obviously meant kill him.
No surprise many of us wear suits.

PROSCRIBED AND SEALED

God's scorekeepers proscribed their fate
    and sealed the gate
Condemned delicious-munching honeymooners
    forced to live beyond paradise.
Keepers hung a No Vacancy sign until
    angels were heard on high.
Outside billboards advertised infallible Fuji-a-day
    become your own God.
Wormwood applauded delightful delicacy.

Of course coarse generation's ignorant arrogantly
    expunged In the beginning.
From hiding place emerged invisible vacancy sign.
    Begin again. Digest the flesh-words.
Words, protested the honeymooners. We need
    protection from flesh-eating banks; we need
    weapons, we need shelter — at least a tent.
    We need a manna-split. We believed a
    Snake-Oil-Slitherer who fleeced us.
    We've been rejected ejected
    marked for extinction

    And you want us to eat words?

ACCURSED QUESTIONS

Who struggles with accursed questions:
    How should one live?
    What is to be done?
    What must we be and do?
Who asks these questions?
    Go to the 19th Century
    Go to Russian writers
    Go to Tolstoy.

If answered by the Tzar, by Stalin,
    The answers cursed millions.

Wrong answers, still the right questions.
    Have to answer now.
When is now?
    Now!

Can't answer without rules.
    Got to have rules!
    So, who sets the rules?
You do!
    I react to rules.
    I don't set them!

You want rules?
Go to the floor of Ngorogoro.
    A pride of lions after breakfast,
    Stretching, yawning.
    Blood stained mouths.
    Shattered bones of a Wilder Beast

Too easy these rules!
      Natural selection,
      Darwin wins!

      Survival of fittest.
      Spencer wins!

How about human rules?
Go to the floor of the Senate.

      A pride of senators after asking
      What is to be done?
      Stretching, yawning.
      Bloated tummies, filler-busted.
      Shattered bones of democracy.

Oligarchy rules create chaos!

Let's try again. How about God's rules?
      Which God: The God of anger, violence?
      Blow the rules and you fry!

How about the God of love, forgiveness?
      Break the rules and ask forgiveness,
      you're still invited to the dance.

Hold it! Which God is in charge?
      The God of forgiveness!

And He provides a get out of jail card?
      There's no free lunch!
      There's always a catch.
      There have to be rules.

You live by ethics not rules.
    Ethics are based on
    Justice and mercy.

What's that mean?
    We're back to I set the rules?

Tougher.
    You have to ask questions!
    Take care of the earth or lose it.
    Take care of yourself.
    Take care of your brother.

Those are the answers to the accursed questions?
    Russia killed people who asked questions.
    They turned plows into gulags.
    Take care of my brother?
    Some fool ate my pension.

STARVED FOR A TOUCH

Separated from earth, worms and dandelions.
Hope smothered, nerves remain on train tracks.
Locked down, buttoned down, nature frowned.
Finally a tattoo proclaims closed for repairs.
Cannot uncouple from the world's fracture.
No attaching to a shooting star!
No healing stations among the neon street signs.
Not even a Greyhound bound for down under.
We gather at the parched river singing,
We're tired and broken, starved for a touch.
Choral response from the other side.
Come on over, we know this much.
Here we have earth, worms and dandelions.
Take a hand and step this way, dare for a touch
And don't look back. We know that much.

NAILED TO THE WORLD'S LAST TREE

I'm told that I will soon be set free. Yet
I wait patiently nailed to the world's last tree.

> I squint as words flash before my eyes.
> Words in neon blue blinking peppermint.
> Saved by blood or saved by declaration
> Life liberty and Happy Meals. Passion
> Words mounted on wings of eagles. They
> Scream Give me Liberty, stay off my property
> The last tree is mine!

I watch chained neighbors taken out to sea.
I listen to passing apocalyptic reproach.

> Have you no mercy he hissed.
> You sneer at us from your lofty perch.
> Yes, we bet on a house of mirror swaps.
> A kingdom for the chosen here on earth.
> Yes, we anted our children and lost the pot.
> We risked to build the gated-new Jerusalem.
> Safe, clean, painted no-stain bright white!
> And you punish us to hope for survival.
> Help us. Come down from the tree.
>
> Keep moving prodded the caryatids.

Who promised to set you free they rant?
What illusion did you sell now you can't.

You promised new life, a new world.
   We wandered and squandered. Oh so
   Easily led by prophets false and gloss, Over-
   Come by flimsy-grace, now anything goes.
   We crossed over, crossed out, double crossed.
   You came with a message to live we must die.
   You said sacrifice abnegate prosperity.
   You said take care of the poor stop the war.

Who beguiled you to promise hope to others?
Whose half-assed plan to seduce our brothers?

   You said enmity and power corrupted is sin.
   Mega-preachers cleared our minds the muddle,
   Power Points enlisted us to shill. Yet you said
   Absorb hostile enemies tear down the walls.
   Who but the anti-Christ would give succor
   To stinking chicken-plucking wetbacks,
   Invite three-year old terrorists to our shores?

Whom did you burn with hope never sent?
Who now condemns you with no relent?

   Your hope forecast is shrouded in dread and agony.
   Our hope protected by tablets now erased and you cry
   Suffer the children orphaned by lepers and whores.
   Don't you know ambivalent borders allowed evil
   Infections to insidiously consume our children.
   We double-quick by your perch on our way to sea
   With cadence of marching feet and beat of drum,
   We have convinced ourselves no life in your tree.

TO EMMAUS

What was that? A groan?

If it was it was sardonic.

How can a groan emit pain
    While mocking—whom? You? Me?
    There! Again! Prolonged.

Where is it coming from?
    Everyone here is dead.

Not it—a legion. Listen carefully.
    A chorus of groans.
    A cacophony crying,
    Your people can't find the virgins.

I hear them. The tone is derisive.

Obviously Jews complaining,
    No rag head to carry their bags.

There. Listen. One voice pleading.
    Not derisive. Forsaken.
    Abandoned. Angry.

Then confronted by a wounded angel
    Where are you going
    You two reprobates?
    You hear the groans

You argue over tone.
Are you deaf? Blind?
You parse words
Amidst blood and bone.
All your people are dead!
And you mock instead?

Jolted by the angry voice,
    Unscrambling nightmares.
    Aghast. Who are you?
    Where did you come from?

    Where are we going?
    Far, far from death.
    To Emmaus!

A Jew, a Muslim together
    On this West Bank road
    Going to sacred sites,
    To find the warrior Judas Maccabees?
    To pray at the Small Mahomeria?

Or are you pursuing miracles on
    This road the disbelieving
    Disciples met their Jesus?

Disoriented the sojourners
    Gasping for breath,
    Grasping for comfort,
    Weeping for hope.
    Are we the survivors?
    Where do we go?
    What do we do?

The angel embraced both
    You are the hope!
    Reconciled you live!
    Stay the road.
    Tell your story.

WHO'S WHO

Who weeps when you suffer?
Who suffers when you can't see a sunset?
Who thunders when you are unjustly maligned?
Who sobs when no one hears your hungry children die?
Who screams Enough, when you are denied entry?
Who urges lovers to love the grossly maimed?
Who asks the poor to forgive the fleecer?
Who prods friends to befriend the abandoned?
Who shakes the oligarch and pleads relief?
Who begs the glacier to refuse carbon's erosion?
Who keeps a hope chest of Not On My Watch signs?
Who is not recognized in the house built for her worship?

HENCE THE LEPIDOPTERAN

Watch multi-colored, wildly patterned butter fly.
    So out of place from another planet,
    So utterly Amazon lost
    Fluttering, withering,
    Announcing salt-free
    Instructions to release
    Gnome capsules buried in
    San Andreas fault.
    Point to Reyes.

Released before plastic surgery,
    There chrysalis perfect.
    Engineered Boeing-free
    No cucumbered eyelids, instead
    A wrapped gold-colored pupa,
    Nympha emerges wings ready.
    Veins haemolymph-filled by angels.
    Color-wheel flutters in the sky.
    Hence, the lepidopteran!

PROSOBUL

Hello, Chase. Devastating news.
He's decided to give debtors a free pass,
forgive their debts.

Who he? The King? What are you talking about?

All debt will be forgiven—everyone who holds a mortgage,
credit card debt, personal loan--a clean slate for every debtor
man, woman, small business. Everyone who owes us.

What? Where'd you hear that nonsense?

The king's going to announce it tonight.

I knew that deluded communist was going to
destroy our cash cows, eat us alive!

There's more. It will become law to clean the slate
every 7 years or every 49 years,
I haven't figured that out yet.

Where's this coming from? He's got to be making this up.
And who is going to believe him?

It's from the Good Book. It's called the Jubilee.
He's got two winners here. One: It comes from the book of
Leviticus in the Old Testament, Bible-thumpers will be
singing Free at Last, and Two, it will free people from their debts.
Who's not going to believe him? He's got to be stopped. But how?

We outsmart him. We always outsmart the social-do-gooders.
We need a meeting of the money-boys.

I'll assemble them. Where?

The Hard Rock for lunch!

But we'll be seen and you know what happens when the peons
think we're planning to increase interest rates!

Nah, they don't go there for lunch. After a breakfast of that
manna-mush they stay away. Can't stand the stuff. Anyway,
have the boys go in through the side entrance, meet in the private
dining room. I'll have management bring up some of our private
stock. And Chase, invite 5 of the High Priests! You know which ones.
What I have in mind we're going to need their pious sanctification
and their protection!

Protection? What are you talking about?

Prosobul.

What's that?

Comes out of the Bible too. It's how the money-lenders figured to sandbag
the king who started all this Jubilee crap.

We're going to be saved by the good book? How does it work pray tell.

We gather up all the big, really big outstanding debts, the bundled mortgages, the twelve figure contracts and have the priests hold 'em until this Jubilee craziness passes. We pay them 10% of total holdings--a tithe not a bribe.

You mean hide the debts?

Hide 'em, hold 'em. If the press starts investigating the priests tell the folks God wants them to hold the debts as the only way to care for the needy, the widows, the orphans. And without the 10% coming from the debts the needy would starve and many would die, so they would be protecting the needy while they really would be protecting our money.

And you think the priests are going to agree?

We own the priests!

And the King? Once he sees what we're doing. You think he's going to fold? We don't own him — do we?

TRICKLE DOWN

Trickle down economics sounds like a bladder problem.
To poor folks trickle down means getting pissed on.
To rich folks trickle down is the politically correct way to say
    Piss on the poor.

WINDOW INTO APATHY

The window streaks red, blood drips,
the diners oblivious, walls shake, all
eat, drink. One armed waiter appears,
tray loaded with ham, eggs and one arm,
his arm. Child follows with bucket
picking up falling debris, flesh.
No one notices. No one, no harm.

Horns blaring, marching band,
majorettes twirling no right arms,
batons flying not returning.
Shorty yelling, table for two.
We got our table, we yell.
Not your table, hurry here come
the trombones. Somebody is
singing, "Have some Madeira
My Dear." Blood everywhere.

My partner asks, "Are we in a
dream?" Everyone now singing,
"Washed in the Blood of
the Lamb." More one arm
people — soldiers, cops,
Girl Scouts. No one asks.
No protests. We all watch.
It is a dream or we are inside
HBO. But we feel nothing.
Those who pass suffer. We
don't suffer. We have no
experience, never did, we

see but don't react. My
partner wants either the
parade or the dream to end.

Then the parade does end,
two clean Shetland ponies,
not a spot of blood on them.
They pull a cart filled with
arms, hands waving as they pass.
I pay the bill and we literally
slip out. The child with the
bucket is at the door asking
for "donations."

SUN SPOTS

Driving the Nairobi/Arusha Highway
destination Kilimanjaro. Nine white
folks being escorted by two Kenyans.
They are introduced as Jim and Randolph.

Rising foothills lead toward Kilimanjaro.
Randolph points toward the verdant foothills.
Carpeted by orchards, vineyards, spring grass.
There, he gestures, look above the vineyard,
there in the grass field. See it?

There a burnt circle — perfectly round — huge!
Wondering aloud at the foothill's mystery,
Randolph interrupts. It's a sun spot. The
sun in certain areas here blisters the
mountain. Nothing grows, the land is
dead and useless.

Sun spot, Randolph added,
like a white man's mind.

SUFFERING SUCCOTASH

If the Looney-Tune's cat with the lisp
actually said "suffering savior"
the cat-in-the-tux cartoon would now
be banned buried under the creche.

Juxtapose the creche with the cross
the swaddling babe to the bloody son,
swap a stuttering cat cameo for Mel's
flesh ripping nails you won't ever
think or hear suffering savior.

You do hear Pontus mega pastors
lisping legal grounds for creches,
Jesus or Barabbas, crosses or creches?
Sweet Jesus of the manger not
bloody suffering Jesus of the cross.

Choose cross and you choose suffering.
Choose suffering you cannot look away
from the cross the poor die on.
This is one strange pussycat tail.
Returning now to suffering succotash

JESUS ON ROLLER SKATES

Dirty-robed bearded man pulling a cross on roller-skates.
Text messages! Homeless guy on roller skates pulling a cross.
Kids scramble on skate boards, bikes, roller blades to find him.
Soon cell phones beep with map coordinates. City of kids
pincher-like surround him to find the cross is on skates.
No matter the word is out, Jesus-Skates go on sale:
Strap 'em on, tie 'em with ribbons, expensive pinks,
fur-lined sheep-herders, sandal-skates for new disciples.
Delivered on site, buy on line, dropped from the sky by
Amazon's new Drone-Drop. Airwaves thumping
the new number one, "Rolling with Jesus." Next day
dirty-robed bearded guy is on Breakfast of Champions
cover wearing roller skates. His agent lined up gigs
throughout the mega-church world. The cross is again the
commercial prop rolled out in front of collection plates.

JOURNEY

the religious journey is a walk through time shares
prepaid stations require travelers to enunciate
tripping on the tongue trifling tautologies.

beyond gloomy internment fields of dying daisies
lilacs parading scents of mind clearings not parked in
endless rows of dark glasses, find one shoot of jesse.

careful not to collect two hundred pesos bypass the litmus,
failures return to begin again, no getting off this tricycle. who
knows the right path, right answer? does the shadow know?

the purveyors of rectitude provide sepulchral prerequisites while
standing on sinking lily pods surrounded by Lillies of the Valley.
we, surrounded by fallen angels and other sweet creations we
embrace bedecked in the glory of morning we set out unrestricted.

ENNUI BAWLERS

Where to sit, always looking for a place to sit.
Cafeteria reeks of classism, racism, jocks-for-Jesus-ism.
Older now cubicle functionary gets twenty minute lunch.
No where to sit, has fewer options, no unique lunch pail.
A table for the listless, the dissatisfied, the don't light my fire.
Bowling gives table meaning, team called the Ennui Bawlers.
Moderate voices dissect our sloth, we are the why generation.
Why? We are children of the entropic age, a spare is heaven.
Crescendos of distaste, disagreement, justification-affirming.
We are children of the sperm bank, DNA hostages, strike that!
We are staged and staffed by listless gods of little imaginations.
Always hope for 300.

DARKED SKINNED JEW

Christian calling pro-Palestinian-
      Israeli, a slimy-skinned Jew.
Jesus was a Jew.
      Was he slimy-skinned?
Being for peace in Middle-Muddle
      is an oxymoronic default
      for born-againsters.

SALINIZED WELL

Such dignity and humility in a leader. I fumble words.
He stood straight frail as if wind would knock him down.
His robe a booboo if I remember grime on white.
Black pupils floating in seas of yellow fever.
      He scans my heart.

You want to know what you can do.
If you see my government,
Tell them to come get their pump
      It never worked.
And I can see you are a spiritual man.
      Pray for rain.

He reveals a rolled leather parchment.
Gently he unravels the scroll.
A list of stick pictures:
      Men with numbers next to them
      many crossed out.
      Women the same.
      Children the same.
      Even livestock.

He leads me to the village well
      Useless he explains as is the pump.
      The Senegal River has become the backwater
      For the Atlantic Ocean.
      The well water is salinized.

Unfortunately he proffers
>	My government
>	is also useless.
>	They cannot make rain.
>	Only Allah can make rain.
>	We obviously offended him.
>	You must pray.

Again the scroll.
>	He hands it to me
>	and a ballpoint pen.
>	Please write your name.

And do not forget my name he demands.

>	I am Mambadu Demba Bah

LOOKING FOR GOD

He's doing his Old Testament,
Evanesces like vapor.
Spent the weekend searching
Church, mosque, synagogue
Asking not-a-clue clerics.

Finally a seer a prophetess
Finger pointing, utters,
God left for the camps
Where he embraces
Parched desolate,
Hopeless children.
The dying.

Camps? God's in Darfur
He abandoned us for
Darfur?

He left a reminder also look for him
Camps Sacramento Seattle Detroit
Under hometown bridges.

No! God's is not exclusive to camps
Look further.

Why not the national day of prayer
They serve God eggs coffee and toast
Pray to Father Son and Holy Ghost.
Look among the elected how

Deniers of God's instructions to
Feed clothe house the poor yet
On this once a year in February
Let's pretend to give a damn
Bow stare at cold eggs and ham.

Camps? Is there a lesson, a point?

There is no future no freedom.

Death wins without emancipation.
God's always been in the camps.

"I have seen the misery of my people
I heard their cry." Camp?
Camp Egypt Camp Babylon
Camp Jerusalem Camp India
Camp South Africa Camp Plantation.
He sent his messengers his liberators.
Moses Jeremiah Esther Mohammed
Gandhi Rose Martin Mandela Jesus

What happened at Auschwitz?
Syria? Rwanda? Kosovo?
A wee shy late Why?

No messengers to answer the cries.
No disciples. They fell asleep.
Again.

And now. Where to find him
Which camp What to do?

Go see with his eyes
Go hear with his ears
Go feed with his hands
Go take water with his feet
Go heal with his heart
You are his bread
You are his water
Go.

COLLECTOR OF PASSIONS

Passions strewn on the floor
Now colorless wedding flower petals
Walked on walked over stuck to soles forgotten
Sacred artifacts I collect them.

Stuff my bag with worthless promissory notes
Now not worth spit so the dark angel would say
I file them anyway under gossamer titles.

    How to end wars How to feed the world
    How to take care of my children all children
    How to rebuild decaying cities How to Jubilee.

Once the bag is stuffed bursting aching to release
I scatter the passion petals on tender soil.
And I spit on 'em to help them grow again.

FLASH-BACKS—FLASH FORWARDS

My nights now have flash-backs and flash-forwards.
The "backs" are often painful, full encounters with dark places, places to ask God to eliminate but not until I have learned from them. Often I stand outside these encounters, they beckon with love signals. Then to "flash-forwards": paint new journeys, new adventures. New! So grateful for my love, for her generous beckoning, for her brave love-hands that stroke me, the children, the world.

ALONE

Making morning coffee for two.
      The demitasse sits empty.
      The house is hollow,
      Me and the ladybug.
      No ladylove of my life.

Again and again, more lonely mornings.
      Same empty cup.
      Same empty space.
      Everywhere reminders of the
      Empty space in my heart.

Come home soon lady-love

PUSH A STAR RIDE A GLACIER

If you're going to push against something,
        push against the stars.
Make a stand? Find a glacier,
        ride it out, hold your position.
Who knows you're there?
Who says you are a great idea?
Who tells you, you need to be heard?
How will you know if your heart's the mother-lode?
You won't learn it in the fast lane.
So push a star, ride a glacier.

RETICULATE

Look down from satellite, or from a starship, perhaps from the moon.

On a clear day you see earth covered with intertwining blue veins.

They mirror an apparition girdling the gracious slow swirling sphere. The blue network webs the globe.

Look at a corpses' skull before embalming; blue veins, rivulets, life's reminder.

We survive on veins, water and blood-webs, these amazing support connections!

See them? Look closely.

A leaf's superstructure is a reticulated architectural masterpiece,

> The veins on the back of your hand, and life rivers —
> Amazon, Mississippi, the Blue and White.

I DRINK FROM AN EMPTY WELL

I drink from an empty well.
Ask the miracle man.
You got water?
    Soon a tanker.
Ah, can I have some?
    Queue!
You mean qui?
    No, queue at the quay
I did that already.
    There must be a hole in your well.
No, I gave away my water
    Then your well isn't empty

INTERSECTIONS

Need total rearrangement. Total!
Intersections are calibrated
To deny freedom
Frustrate creative growth.

They are without competition
For meeting yesterday's expectations
Look at a section of the city map
There it is, the corners of . . . fill in the names
Or more supercilious fill in the numbers
Now remember you live at N.E. 145th at 9th Ave West.

To be a mad scientist an inventor
A diviner of water a prophet of repute
Who will take you seriously with that address?
You're in a box at an intersection defined by
Systems and structures and sequences.

Write that on a job application
Chances are the postman will find you.
He'll post "Thanks for coming in
But we have filled our void."

But why Who?

A Zebra-riding GIS scientist got the job!

OK, so what's his address?

She lives on Columbus Circle

What's all this got to do with intersections?

If you live in the mind of an intersection,
You are an intersection.
You're locked down in the grid of city
No getting out.

OK OK how do I get out?
How do I create an alternative
Live on a circle?

Get a Zebra!

IRONIC PARAMETERS

Heart broken by sunlight
Hearing clogged by tears
Sight clouded by thunder
Led by a seeing-eye mole

Destination is darkness
Crutches for giraffes
Banal signposts
Left by virtual heroes

Truth carved in brimstone
Wounds with no blood
Children with candles
Parading in the wind

Sinking to the surface
Water walk catch lightning
Irony in the meaning
Star in the morning.

WHO HEARS MY HEART

What does the falcon hear
when summoned to the arm of
the falconer? What pricks the
memory? Master? Meat? Taste of
blood?

Who hears my heart thumping?
Fear scared by shadowy manikin targets,
my band of 'we hear you' brothers,
pass the nachos. If no one hears
how do I find home? How does
the falcon find the glove
holding raw meat?

No name here, blank tag.
Rather have a nom de guerre,
so hidden in the basement with
the dead soldiers long forgotten
yet known as roving, wandering
foreign to nachos, migratory
Peregrine. My eponym now
hooded found the glove.

TASTE THE TEARS

Woke in darkness scary-chills alert!
Somebody in the room, on the ceiling?
The sounds the sobs coming from where?
Sobs? Somebody crying. Heart-wrenching.
Can't hear now, back up the sound track.
Dream! Can't remember but the chill is back.
One you don't want to replay because
   It scares the hell out of you!

Nodding off again attempting to shutter.
The mind returns to the dream. Failing. Falling.
Sobbing. Again. Emitting pain unknown.
Despair beyond my reach. Not so much
Frightening as uncontrollable. Who knows
Such agony so disconsolate? Who?
   Why in my dream?

For heaven's sake screamed the vapor,
The sobbing is happening in a thousand dreams,
In the dreams of all you say-so redeemed!
The sobbing is for the children of the damned!
The wailing is for the helpless, the homeless,
The heaped bodies endless rows of crucifixions.
The sobbing is for the poor who keep sacrificing.
And the crying is for you the say-so who don't.
   Taste the tears, they're from God.

FALLING LEAVES

What do you see when the autumn leaf falls?
    A rake?
    A pile to jump in?
    The leaf more exquisite
    In death than life.

PRAY AND PARK

How to stop wars, AIDS, poverty!
Call for a national day of prayer.
Invite only those who pray for and
 get parking places.

CHERISHED

There we are, sitting talking nothings,
Feelings transitory, oblivious, tongues dulled.
She streams tears, sunken shrunken.
    You no longer cherish me.
    Where do you go? You disappear.
    You stare at me eyes mummified.
    I lost you, can't reach you.
Talk to me or lose me, she mutters.
Quicksand with no ladder, I stutter.

You can't help me—I whisper.
    You won't let me, she says.
I hear only what is threatening;
    She sobs, trembling—
    Let me in.

Where do I go when I go inside?
    So many doors with
    Do Not Enter signs.
    I've stuffed the rooms with
    Junk—fears, abuses, secrets.

Again, to her and myself,
    You can't help me, I whisper.
    Again she says, You won't let me!

Why go there?
>   Truth suffocates in dark places.
>   No one could tell I was hiding,
>   Let's pretend in a Blazer.
>   Mirage on my own desert.

But she knows, has forever.
>   She flowers my desert.
>   She won't give up.
>   I am her cherished.
>   Come out she sings,
>   Come out wherever you are.

SING THE WIND'S HOSANNA

Walking the path to
    farmstead's memory.
Carpets of wild flowers
    sweet pastels petal by.
Spring Beauty fringes
    kiss the wild raspberries;
Strawberries creep
    hinting blushes of fruit.
Fox Glove sentries,
    taps from a thousand bugles
The path bends
    to the tall gates
    reaching to the taller Firs.
They tangle at
    cloud's wisp
    blue ceiling,
Enter the cathedral,
    sing the wind's hosanna!
All the senses
    sing multiple-color harmony.
    All searching ends here.

THERE WALKS HOPE

    Abraham, according to the Apostle Paul,
        Against hope,
        Believed with hope.
    According to a modern writer
        Hope is dark
        Like to muddy waters.
    According to a modern group
        Hope is Dead!
    Stop looking outside.
        Look inside for answers.
        Just hope it's not dark in there.

    We thirst for hope.

    There walks hope. Clear as a burning bush.
    There, a girl raised in Darfur decades past.
        She was kidnapped, raped, tortured.
        That was dark, bleak no-hope.
        She escaped, became a nun,
        Returned to Darfur to serve,
        to love, to shine her light on
        hopeless children.

    Recently, Sister Josiphine Bakhitd was
        Named Saint Josiphine.
        How did that happen?
        Was not hope so buried,
        So covered with the feces of denial,
        So obscured by the stank of death's breath?
        Yet to discover healing and resurrection;
        then plant hope back in rape's bed!

There goes hope again.
        Clear voice calling,
        Break the chain.

The Khmer Rouge captured him,
        sentenced him to death.
        A young Cambodian farmer
        who became a warrior
        fighting for freedom
        against the killer Pol Pot.

Finally surrounded and surrendered,
        ankles chained to a post,
        night brought hope.

Break the chain, said the voice!
        Again and again,
        Break the Chain.
        He did! and escaped
        to the Thai border,
        to a refugee camp.

Who was the Voice? Who freed him?
Who gave him the power to break the chain?
Hope walking now, hope giving hope,
        Removing chains now from
        his peoples' hearts and ankles.

To believe with hope,
        One must look to see hope walking.
        One must adjust ones ears to hear
        Chain breaking!

To believe with hope,
>One must understand
>Hope is the most subversive
>Demonstration of God's
>Love and Justice!

THE SILVER-HAIRED SOCIALIST ARISTOCRAT

When a graduate student in New Jersey

I knew an elegant gentleman,
    a silver-haired socialist aristocrat
    a guide who poked, prodded, encouraged.
His primary message
    Attain the unattainable!

His constant reminders:
    Study! Work hard! Prepare!
    Take care of the people around you!

As the friendship grew the instructions got tougher:
    You're not asking the right questions!
    You're world is too small!
        Read the NY Times, New Yorker, Daily Worker
        Listen to Sibelius, Pete Seeger, Lena Horne, Monk.
        Go see plays by Miller and Shakespeare.
        Read the speeches of Martin and Malcolm.
        Read Locke, Tolstoy, Illich, Marshall, Buckley, Baldwin,
        Dorothy Day and his favorite Niebuhr.

He challenged and enlarged my safe world:
    Ben Shahn is coming over tomorrow. You be here!
    Ben Shahn paintings are throughout the mansion.
    His Hebrew alphabet goes up the staircase
    At the top of the stairs the Saccho and Vanzetti poster.

The silver fox sprinkled little wisdom-gems I didn't understand then
    Don't let them spoil you.
    Don't let them tell you who you are.
    Don't let them tell you what you believe.

What do I remember about the man
    He radiated enthusiasm for life—at 80 plus years
    He sat majestically on his four-poster propped on pillows
    Tweed jacket bright purple button-down and orange tie,
        Surrounded by Times editorials and yellow pads
        A delicate flower in his lapel.

Come sit beside me:
    Tell me about your day, how is the world?
    How did it treat you today? How did you treat it?

    Beneath the white crew cut and flagship eyebrows
        Blue eyes twinkle with joy to see friends
        Heart attacks did not quell his passions.

    He lost his fortune during the great Wall Street crash.
    It savaged all his riches—his international bank
        his railroad, his servants, it took everything
        But it did not steal his will to thrive.
    His favorite response to those fatal days
        I gave it all including me to the Carpenter
        Told Jesus I would work to make the world better for all
        especially those without voice and that's what I've attempted
        to do.

He ran as the socialist candidate for Governor in Jersey.
He joined the committee to disband HUAC.
He organized Boys Clubs in several cities.
He opened his home to writers, artists, musicians,
students, union leaders, teachers, liberals, conservatives.
We sat at his feet and listened and laughed and learned.
We lingered until each could be touched and be blessed.
Never a goodbye rather
Take a smile to a child . . .

CARE-TAKING — BY CROW

Don't feed the crows. Don't start!
Well, we did start, feed them daily.
Walk out the door onto porch and a
congregation suddenly appear
on rooftops, branches, squawking.
Thrown crumbs create chaos until
pecking orders are screamed from the
dive bomber who scatters poachers.
The grand diva and her protector
descend stuff their beaks before liftoff
leaving a patchwork of leftovers for
their offspring, almost a biblical
picture of gleaning.

The diva and her mate are friends.
Certainly not pets. They are too wise
too wily to trade tricks for treats.
After months of watching, testing,
deciding we were not threats, they
created a "no fly zone," around our
bungalow, it seemed only their crow
family and friends were allowed.
No name-tags but we can identity
by characteristic, behavior, and
feather arrangements — crow
fashion show on a green carpet.

I was stunned when invited to a
death-watch for one crow. We had
watched him, he limped, one wing

dragging on the ground. He struggled
to fly. He would often set down
below the window of my study
nestled by the fence.

One morning he lay there
surrounded by three crows
including the diva. I went
to inspect and saw he was

dying, neck stretched,
panting. I watched from my
window. He suffered for two
days. His family tended to him,
a hospice-nest, brought food,
stood guard, allowed me to
bring water, to sit close.

Death followed by gifts of
twigs and grass. Later I picked
him up by shovel. Nothing but
feathers, no weight. I carried
him to the compost pile, laid
him out as his family circled.

The tribe seems to know my
cancer is erupting again. They
bring small gifts — get-well
cards — strings, clam shells,
twigs, petals —place them on
the path to my backyard study.

GOD'S GARDEN IN THE DESERT

God's people according to the Book
spent many years wandering in the desert.
Often abandoned because of disobedience
they suffered, parched, pleaded for water.
Always dreaded the answer to how long.
O Lord's answer — more pain required.

So Eden was messed up and we're
condemned to wander sun-blistered
through eternity? Got to blame somebody.
We are oblivious to rules established by
dead prophets — do justice? love kindly?
be humble? These will get us out of the
desert to fresh water?

Pivot! Wander into draught-death camp.
Several refugee survival-stations surround
the literal valley of the shadow of death.
Hundreds dying daily! Thousands arrive
from Eritrea, from throughout northern
Ethiopia. Once in the camps many saved,
no one counts the dead, the to-be buried.
Typhus rips children from mother's breast.
Still not enough pain, O Lord?

Not to worry, yells the camp doctor.
We've got this covered, soon no more
deaths. We will heal and return the
near-dead to their villages. And then
the shock! Come, I want to show you
my garden!

We are not watching a tv documentary.
Rather, we are in a triage tent where decisions
are made, who lives who dies, where this raving
doctor is screaming at us to take a walk with
him to see his garden, his oasis of life!
Could have been Moses explaining that
water would sprout from local rocks. Right!

So eager to escape the death tent we
would follow the crazed doc into hell.
We did! He led to the valley floor, a
furnaced dust-bowl sitting below the
camps. A living post card from Gomorra.
Our group from the states begins to lose it:
I'm too rich for this, get me out of here;
another —I need a stiff drink! Sobbing.
Dry heaves. What's next? Lions? Daniel
coming? From inside our group, Get a grip,
people are dying here!

The scorched desert respects no one, the
sun blisters white and black lips, red spills
from abscesses Muslim, Christian, Falasha.
Tongues swell stifling help pleas for Water!
Allah, Yahweh, Jesu — no response.

Ah, but there is water responds the
crazy doc! Gather round me!
Closer! In a circle. Listen and watch.
These dear people are starving, they

are dying from thirst. Sending money
ain't gonna solve this. We've just enough
now for a month's worth of wheat and water.
Next month you gotta send more. Our visitors
from the states are getting nervous. One
CEO smirks, says he wants to get out. The
crazy doc points toward the bruising
sandstorm behind us. Be my guest.
You want to go back to Pharaoh,
take my camel!

Crazy continued, What do you need to
grow a garden? Silence. C'mon folks.
You need sun, got lots of it here. You
need dirt. Little dry but lots of it. And
you need — pause — he choked —
Water! Yep, as I said, there is water.
And it's right under your feet!

Crazy swept sand from boards covering
a well. He picked up an attached rope
that disappeared into the hole, pulled
until a small bucket appeared, full
of water — clean, fresh water. He
cupped his hand dipped it in the
bucket, pulled it to his mouth and
drank!

Now, sang Crazy, we got the
makings of a beautiful garden!

WHAT WORTH A MAN AT 80

I have a friend, kind, wonderful,
    loves and is loved by dirt.
He stirs the soil with magic fingers,
    the earth kisses him with
    beautiful petal on stem.

He surprised me weeks back,
    while doing coffee,
    a Saturday meet
    at Adelaide's,
    saying,

Once you're no longer a
    producer, no longer
    an income creator,
    you're not worth much

My response: Bull Shite!
    The BS response
    was loud, startled
    my friend, and
    nearby patrons!

If you followed my friend
    walking through
    Jack's, the stacks
    at the library,
    crafting sculptures
    at Bay Ave. Gallery,
    greeting at the Methodist
    church, on and on,

it's like the opening song
        on Cheers, Everybody
        knows your name . . .
The difference here is my
        friend knows every
        soul he encounters,
        By name!

Amazing! To be addressed
        by name is such bounty.
        Folks carry burdens,
        grief, sadness, some
        with joys to share,
        their friends long
        taken.

Hello, with a name attached
        is the most profound
        ministry. My friend,
        the walking Rolodex.

What are you worth, at 80?
        More than a Potosi mine,
        a Wall Street bell ringer.

Carry on, dear friend.
        And that's no BS!

SIXTY

60! Married for sixty years!

> 60 years! how long is . . . ?
> 720 months! 260 birthday
> cards from grandma!
> 23 moves, 1,247 shoes,
> 165 stitches, and everyone
> ran away from home
> at least once
>
> Married? wed, yoked;
> Through rain, snow, sleet;
> Wrong vow: Rather, to have
> and to hold from this day forward . . .
>
> I like the Apache vows for us:

"Now you will feel no rain,
for each of you will be shelter for the other.
Now you will feel no cold,
for each of you will be warmth for the other.
Now there will be no loneliness,
for each of you will be companion to the other.
Now you are two persons, but there is only
one life before you."

60 going on 70 — it's been a joyful romp
and miles to go . . .

www.ingramcontent.com/pod-product-compliance
Lightning Source LLC
Chambersburg PA
CBHW060203050426
42446CB00013B/2967